Hurting God

Part Essay Part Rhyme

RITA ANN HIGGINS

salmonpoetry

Published in 2010 by
Salmon Poetry
Cliffs of Moher, County Clare, Ireland
Website: www.salmonpoetry.com
Email: info@salmonpoetry.com

ISBN 978-1-907056-51-2

Cover photography/image by *Bernadette Higgins*
Cover design & typesetting by *Siobhán Hutson*
Printed by imprint*digital*.net

Salmon Poetry receives financial assistance from the Arts Council

for Christy Higgins

Acknowledgements

Grateful acknowledgements to the editors of the following, where some of these essays or poems first appeared:

'Be Someone' first appeared in the collection *Witch in the Bushes* (Salmon Publishing, 1988 & 1993). It subsequently appeared in *Throw in the Vowels: New & Selected Poems* (Bloodaxe, 2005, reissued in 2010 with audio CD).

'Bóithrín and Bog' first appeared in *The Irish Times* on August 22nd, 2005 under the title 'Finding a new world in the west'.

'Borders' first appeared in the *Oxfam Poetry Calendar* 2007.

A different version of 'Brides of The Stitch 'n Times' was broadcast on *Sunday Miscellany* (RTE Radio 1) in December 2009 under the title 'Turkey Time'.

The 'Malaga O' Malaga' essay and poem first appeared in *Sonas – Celtic Thoughts on Happiness*, edited by Catherine Conlon (Hachette Books Ireland, 2009).

'The Priest is Coming We Can Feel It in Our Bones' first appeared in *Higher Purchase* (Salmon Publishing, 1996).

'This Was No Ithaca' first appeared in *Poetry Ireland Review* Issue 99.

'Toronto Interlude' first appeared in *Poetry: Reading it, Writing it, Publishing it*, edited by Jessie Lendennie (Salmon Poetry, 2009)

'When the Big Boys Pulled Out' first appeared in the collection *Higher Purchase* (Salmon Publishing, 1996). It subsequently appeared in *Throw in the Vowels: New & Selected Poems* (Bloodaxe, 2005, reissued in 2010 with audio CD).

'Ask the Concierge', 'Borders', 'Malaga O' Malaga', 'This Was No Ithaca', 'Unadorned' and 'The Púca' will appear in Rita Ann Higgins's new collection of poetry, *Ireland Is Changing Mother*, to be published by Bloodaxe in 2011.

The author would like to thank Jessie Lendennie, Siobhán Hutson, Eva Bourke, Mary Dempsey, Heather Higgins, Jennifer Higgins, Maura Kennedy, and Neil Astley.

'There is a superstition in avoiding superstition'

FRANCIS BACON, 1561-1626

'The Devil watches all opportunities'

WILLIAM CONGREVE, 1670-1729

'That's the problem with people, they are always en route to somewhere, why can't they just sit still and enjoy the emptiness. A bit of emptiness never killed anyone.'

ELLEN *in* FACE LICKER COME HOME,
a play by Rita Ann Higgins (Salmon Publishing, 1991)

Contents

Introduction

Rita Ann Higgins has always been an iconoclastic poet of the underclass, an unforgettable voice in a nation teeming with literary talent. Even among Irish writers who celebrate rebellion, even in a culture that venerates eloquent defences of the disenfranchised, Rita Ann Higgins's poetry stands out. In the works in this collection, we are reminded of how singular she remains, for her 'burnt-thistle thoughts', her artful ventriloquisms, and her darkly playful jabs. As she confesses in her essay 'The Faraways': 'I'm a disturber'. For, while Irish society, historically, allocates special status for the bard as a moral compass for the community, Rita Ann Higgins ruefully reminds us, for 'some people', 'poetry doesn't pay'.

In *Hurting God*, we are treated to a new and delightful pairing of poetry and impressionistic vignettes of reminiscence. This coupling – 'part essay, part rhyme' – allows Higgins to showcase both fresh and familiar themes while conveying the fierce, black humour for which she is so well known. Especially enchanting for long-time readers of Rita Ann Higgins's work are those essays that lull us into thinking we are sharing a pot of tea, as she muses over an old poem or, rarer still, teases out an image or a stanza to blossom before our eyes. 'Toronto Interlude', for example, helps us glimpse how she depends upon what we might call her 'inward ear' to launch a lyric: the poem begins 'when words have a ping in their step, or when sounds evoke a memory that may be long forgotten'.

Rita Ann Higgins is immediately recognisable, even amidst the crowd of contemporary Irish poets, for her acerbic catalogue of grievances regarding 'the welfare crowd', as well as her incantatory litanies for the 'women of Baile Crua' or 'the brides of the stitch 'n time'. Equally central to Higgins's poetry is her impressionistic evocation of the West of Ireland, from Galway's bustling Eyre Square to the serenity of her cottage on Galway Bay. No matter the location, Higgins provides us with a vivid cast of characters: the devout church ladies polishing brass for 'their loving Godling', a father who lilts in Irish and rages in English, the chattering shirt factory girls, with their 'blade-like' repartee, the pheasant sisters and the fox. Attentive to the cadence of conversation, the lyricism of insults and jokes, exhaustively curious about even the least sympathetic of passing people, Rita Ann Higgins is inevitably drawn to dramatic monologues, which allow her to artfully mimic voices that we rarely hear in contemporary Irish verse. Like Robert Browning, whose most masterful dramatic monologues satirise the viewpoints of religious hypocrites and patrician misogynists, Rita Ann Higgins uses the form to exquisite effect, whether in satirically 'mimicking a father', as comfort and entertainment for her siblings, in 'Be Someone', or in skewering the self-importance of the 'Flash Harry' doorman she encounters in Toronto.

In 'The Faraways', Higgins tells us, 'You have to remember where you came from so that you will know how to go back', and this collection provides ample opportunities for us to return to Higgins's cultural, geographic, religious, and class origins: back gardens in Baile Crua; rhapsodising, Irish-speaking relatives in southern Connemara; cacophonous streets in the Mervue council estates. In an interview, Higgins has affectionately recalled that 'I had great security in knowing the mammy was there for me' ('Devil'). Not surprisingly, her mother makes many appearances in this collection.

While her father was barely visible in her earliest volumes, his voice and his character have become increasingly prominent in her most recent collections, possibly because, as Rita Ann gently concedes, she didn't get on with him until he died ('Devil'). Raised in Leitir Móir, in Irish-speaking Connemara, her father discouraged his children from learning what he considered 'that poverty language'. Yet, Higgins implicitly acknowledges in the essays that follow that the rhythm and inflection of her lyrics are deeply informed by his irrepressible singing, just as her acid idiom owes a debt to his querulous tongue. Her fleeting contact with the Irish language – 'full of sing, full of sorrow' – proved an influential, if mystifying experience: it was 'a Sunday language without the holy water and a priest with foul breath'. Even as it was banished from the Higgins home, this guttural tongue made a lasting impression on her poetic sensibility: 'I couldn't reach any of it but I loved all of it'. In her desire to learn, listen to, and speak in his native tongue, she is forced to reconsider memories of his past together with hers. This return to her father's first language proved 'a pivotal force' for Higgins in selecting a cottage in Spiddal, in view of the Aran Islands, where J.M. Synge travelled a century earlier to 'express a life that has never found expression' in the medium of English.

Throughout this collection, we can see that Rita Ann Higgins has stayed, in her words, 'true to the subversive' ('True'). In the poems and essays that follow, Higgins returns to Eyre Square and the Mervue council estates, designed by city planners to ensure that Irish rebel names would be 'remembered forever', though the nationalist ambition to cherish 'all of the children of the nation equally' has gone largely unfulfilled. It is her working-class origins that prompt her sceptical, often biting treatment of individuals and institutions – multinational firms, misogynistic men, compassionless nuns – that degrade and humiliate those without the privileges of power, money, and influence. As Rita Ann Higgins's reputation has grown, her poetry has examined the human condition from an increasingly global perspective, one that embraces the exchanges and growth that come from new cultures and traditions. As she explains, 'We were alone for nine hundred years / now all those loving collisions' ('Malaga'). We follow her to Dresden and share in her shocked mourning, as she learns of the murder of her brother, who was working in Saudi Arabia. We can people-watch with her at a Spanish airport, as visitors reunite en route to holidays on the Costa de Sol. And we are privy to her sly, caustic commentary on the slavish, tip-seeking Toronto doorman, whose message to visitors lacking Gucci-labelled luggage is the same that the city dispenses to its homeless: 'My name is zero tolerance, have you a license for that rig?' ('Ask the Concierge').

Still, as Rita Ann Higgins's travels have taken her across Europe, to Asia, and around the States, the journey that might be most surprising is the one back to her rural, Irish-speaking second home in Spiddal, on the Galway Bay. Perhaps we have her cottage to thank for some of her most tender, perceptive work. No one can doubt the emotional range of Higgins's writings after she encourages us to contemplate the infinite variations in human hugs ('Malaga') or reveals the hollow ache in meeting her brother's casket at Shannon airport ('Unadorned'). While Rita Ann Higgins has avowed that she lacks the vocabulary for landscape poetry, her lyricism flowers most movingly when she evokes her bucolic new idyll in 'Pheasantville'. Listening to the tuneful songbirds, eavesdropping on the casual exchanges among Irish-speaking families, and, significantly, joining the 'ciorcal cómhrá' [Irish conversational circle] held weekly down the lane, Rita Ann Higgins has become 'the woman from Prospect Hill', full of deep contentment in her close quarters, hushed by stillness, dreaming up quiet, reflective observations and delicate poems that may be some of her most rewarding work to date.

KAREN STEELE
Professor of English and Women's Studies
Texas Christian University, Fort Worth, Texas
August 2010

SELECTED READINGS ABOUT RITA ANN HIGGINS

Gilsenan Nordin, Irene. "True to the Subversive': Rita Ann Higgins in Conversation.' *Nordic Irish Studies* 6.(2007): 133-141.

Hildebidle, John. "I'll Have to Stop Thinking About Sex': Rita Ann Higgins and the 'Patriarchal Tradition'.' *Contemporary Irish Women Poets: Some Male Perspectives*. 33-41. Westport, CT: Greenwood, 1999.

Paul, Catherine. 'Rita Ann Higgins: A Moderator's View.' *South Carolina Review* 32.1 (1999): 12-14.

Steele, Karen. 'Devil in the Mirror.' *Irish Literary Supplement: A Review of Irish Books* 20.2 (2001): 15-16.

--. 'Refusing the Poisoned Chalice: The Sexual Politics of Rita Ann Higgins and Paula Meehan.' *Homemaking: Women Writers and the Politics and Poetics of Home*. 312-333. New York: Garland, 1996.

Hurting God

"The changes are going to be great in Baile Crua,"[1] I heard my mother say to a neighbour when they were out pegging clothes. I handed up the pegs. They had the same colours as the hen rings, bright reds and yellows. Shirt after shirt, peg after peg. Red with red, yellow with yellow.

Septic tank talk was all talk and if it wasn't septic tanks it was County Council talk. The County Council men played cards a lot, they had a flair for it, and while they played they sang in unison "....From a Jack to a King/ from Loneliness to a Wedding Ring...." The county council men were fixers, they fixed everything from a warped wheelbarrow to a broken scullery window. But they were slow and everyone seemed to be waiting for them. Are you going to the dispensary, Missus? No I'm waiting for the County Council to come and fix a leak in my gutter.

My sister made a daisy-chain so long that it went around the twelve cottages twice and its shadow was nearly as long. When she was threading it she squinted one eye like a shooter in the cowboy films. She said a gecko flitted on the back of her daisy-chain, never falling off once all the way round.

None of us could swim yet, but one brother often jumped into the green slimy tank water to catch the tadpoles. The others trapped wasps in jam jars and broke the odd scullery window. Chase games were always better than hopscotch. We were chased and we chased all day long, losing sight of what we were running after or who was running after us. The boys played hurling and football.

A State of Grace was what we all wanted; we didn't understand it, but we heard it so often that we knew we must have it. I'll have a State of Grace and chips please. My mother was afraid of drunken doughnuts, especially a falling-down father doughnut who brought the house and the dresser down with him. A holy house is falling down falling down falling down. I am in the bottom of the dresser and afraid is there too. I want to go to the toilet.

Now everyone was talking about the changes. Even the postman said, "Did you see that washing machine in full wallop? All your sins will be washed clean." This was bungalow time. A nice house for the teacher and the guard, a bungalow for the little bald man who shot the melaka out of cats. The new word for saying over and over. Bungalow, bungalow. Next thing you know the middle house has venetian blinds. Any day now a president will get shot and the mothers of Baile Crua will cry.

All this carry on was hurting God. I knew by the look on my mother's face. She had a hurting God look, she wore it often. When cousin Patsy came out to visit wearing her black slacks, I knew by the look on my mother's face that she was hurting God.

God was crucified by bungalows and washing machines, and venetian blinds and by tight slacks on women. We had the Stanley Nine but none of the other God-hurting stuff. But it was our fault, it was my fault. I was guilty.

"Take this note to the Poor Clares. Hold it tight and here is one brother and one sister to walk each side of you to shield you from the devil in case he pops up and offers you venetian blinds or a new bungalow or a washing machine on full cycle. The devil is everywhere, remember that."

The note said, pray like billy-o for a father's drinking. A father who fell off the Honda 50 at the gable end was covered in blood. Children scatter, a hailstorm of summer dresses and short pants. I run in to my hiding place in the dresser. Veronica wipes the Honda 50.

At the Poor Clares convent the nuns had a vow of silence, except the nun who would slide back the little net screen. She would take your note, say a few words, all small words, spare the butter words, whispery words with cobwebs. One of us said she had a mouth like a hen's hole but we were well away from the convent by then. We burst in laughing.

Out there someone was going to shoot a president. The mammies in Baile Crua were getting ready to cry. On your marks, get set, a president is about to die.

The whispering nun was roly-poly and she nearly rolled over my brother. She brought us a holy trinket, a thread from Saint Martin's underpants. Or a sliver from Padre Pio's mitten. We didn't care what we got as long as we got something. If we got nothing it would have been a complete waste of a journey in from Baile Crua. *Hail Holy Queen Mother of thirsty, give me a drink and make it hurt me.*

"Hold this note in your other hand. When you finish in the Poor Clares, go to Wood Quay and give it to Paddy O'Flynn and he will put the box of groceries into the back of Mr Kane's van and tell him not to forget the lard or I'll make lard out of ye. Then ye will go with the groceries and he will bring ye home. And God keep ye safe and protect ye from all harm."

But first Paddy O'Flynn always gave you a free Turkish Delight bar and one each for your angels and guardians. That was much better than a saint's relic. With the saint's relic you made the sign of the cross on your forehead and nothing much happened but with the Turkish Delight, you could dream a whole country up, where people spent the day making a special purple bar for you and your minders.

You could see old men in the back of Paddy O'Flynn's licking the top of a big glass of porter and saying nothing. Like the nuns, they had taken a vow of silence. Now and then they looked out at the bacon slicer taking skelps off a side of bacon. These were the saddest men in the world, and they were born old with nothing but big grey eyes and purple noses, like a father.

Mr Kane had no face, only the back of a head. A hair-oiled head and two ears. In the back of his delivery van we'd sway back and forth and we'd laugh when the van went over a bump in the road. Mr Kane couldn't say funny things like a father but he could say things with a soft voice like a nice person. He was a never-learned-how-to-shout person.

The trees move past us and the well moved down the road and Mrs Coyne's house just floated away and everything in it floated out, and the shoes came out from under the beds and odd socks found their long-lost companions only to lose them again, and ladies' nylons and corsets were floating and dancing and bread and jam was flying past the window and fried bread dipped in egg and buttermilk and blackberries and hazelnuts, and the butter was beating off the sides of the churn and the bungalows and the venetian blinds were floating and all the new washing machines were on full cycle. I think I said stop, but it might be a lie. God forgive me.

When we got out at our house, I vomited the whole Poor Clares day into my good shoes. By now a president was dead. The mammies of Baile Crua were all crying. I needed the County Council to come and fix things but I knew deep down that a card game was in full swing. I could hear the men sing in unison, "....From a Jack to a King/ From loneliness to a wedding ring...." I knew that I was hurting God and that I would have to pay, sooner or sooner.

This Was No Ithaca

The women of Baile Crua
never filled their heads
with yellow and pink rollers
letting on to be going somewhere
when there was no somewhere to go.

Somewhere was where other women went
women with magnolia vision
and pencil-shaped dreams
and always a jezebel cigarette
between those blood-red lips.

The women of Baile Crua
filled their heads
with a loving Godling
whom they duly served
every waking second.

They implored their loving Godling
to follow their vagabond sons
down the alleyways of Cricklewood
and Camden Town and further afield.

If the pencil shapers
turned the heads of the husbands
and if the husbands called out the wrong name
when they were claiming their God-given rights,
what harm was it for God's sake.

It was fine with the women
who never filled their heads
with yellow and pink rollers
and never let on to be going somewhere
when there was no somewhere to go.

These women were busy imploring
their loving Godling
to keep their daughters in a state of grace
until the wedding night
and not allow shame to fall on the family
by letting any daughter of theirs
waddle down the aisle
with a belly full of baby.

For the favours sought from
their loving Godling
the women with no rollers
would wear their knuckles inside out,
making God's altar shine.

And God's marble was a sheet of ice
and the husbands whose heads were
pencil-shaped turned,
saw themselves in it when they went up
to receive the body of Christ.

The women of Baile Crua
made many sacrifices,
and the deity was always the same,
their own Godling.

He kept them on their toes
they praised him often
at doorsteps with arms folded
at bus stops and at the solemn novena
and any place that resembled a cross,
ditch, bóithrín or bog.

Except for Missus-All-Over-Hurt
who had no deity that wasn't
in a small brown bottle
that brought instant rapture
when she tossed three or four
of them beauties onto her palm.
They took away the rasping pain
of the day the other women's God
let her only son kiss the face of a raging truck.

This was no Ithaca,
no sweat was ever broken
trying to reach here.
You could get here by taking
a bus from Eyre Square
and collecting your parked bike
from a friend's garden
and cycle the last mile.

There was no Poseidon here
to blow a hole in your dreams,
this was a place you didn't need
rollers in your hair for,
letting on to be going somewhere
where there was no somewhere to go.

This was Baile Crua
all you needed was a loving Godling
to polish and die for.

The Darkness

There was nothing but bleakness, not even a scrawny dog was left, not even a burnt thistle. This was your thought, or at least the thought that came back to you with its enabler, fear.

You looked up the road and down the road and it wasn't even a road it was somewhere your feet happened to be standing on: the ground felt singed under your feet. This was emptiness. You didn't boil an egg for it, but you didn't throw it out with the dirty potato water either. It stayed when you kept it there. When you let it go, it went, but it was sly and it would creep back sometimes when the May flowers were out and there was no call for it.

Nighttimes were treacle black. They haunted little children and big men. Dogs stayed under the range with their heads down. Outdoors was for spectres and hoofed creatures that had strange powers. Children of the long-legged day, look out and be petrified. The darkness was there and darkness mattered. The dark was a talking point; it middled and ended things just like the weather or sickness. No one talked about what if there was nothing but nothingness. So I kept that secret a secret. Wipe that straois[2] off your face and keep your nothingness to yourself.

Out of the darkness came an old couple. They stood at the end of our garden. She had long grey hair; it grew in front of us. He wore rags and his fingers were all cut. His eyes had children in them. Don't look out after dark. Don't give emptiness a boiled egg, and don't throw dirty water at it.

When the stars were out the old man and his wife faded into the bushes where the clucking hen settled. The old man cut his fingers making a way through the briars for her long, grey hair. Her bare feet never touched the ground.

Soon the hens will be out, so will the geese and the ducks. Red wool is being bought for your new jumper. You are getting bigger ever day; your aunts say so when they visit on Sundays. The emptiness comes and goes but you have no word for it. What word could you call it and who could you tell?

Grown-ups talked about illness, awful day, how's Paddy's hernia? Veins were commonplace; every second person had vein trouble. How in God's name is she? Not too bad, she had the veins done last week. She has to walk ten miles a day after them. The women here were good friends. They stuck together, but they wouldn't have the time to walk ten miles a day. What with polishing the altar for their loving Godling, and all the time they spent out pegging clothes.

Where would they find the time to scratch themselves? They would never do that anyway because they were ladies, and you would hear it said often, she was a lady. It was the last word as far as compliments went.

Anyone who cursed was a trollop or a striapach[3] and anyone who used Our Lord's name in vain had no class. This rule seemed to apply to women only because men swore all the time.

And out of the darkness came all the burnt thistle thoughts you have ever had and they frog-marched each other right into your dreams and they landed, one on top of the other. The fittest coming to the fore and facing you down. Child of nine, your thoughts are mine. I own you. I am misery, marry me.

Signs were everything and scratching meant that you either had fleas or lice. The fleas were as common as the veins. Something called 'Flack' was sprinkled on the sheets. It was a white powder with a sulphury smell. It killed the fleas stone dead; that you were breathing it in all night every night didn't matter, at least you weren't scratching in public.

Head lice was the worst kind of bad social background giveaway. "Did you see her up at the altar making a holy show of herself scratching?"

Our lice never got that far, as our heads were doused with paraffin oil and the fine combing done onto a newspaper by a father before we left the house.

God was thanked many times a day and every birthmark was blessed. 'God bless the mark' was said over and over and 'Thank God' was said for everything from a nice blue ribbon to news about an improvement in a neighbour's illness. There's been an improvement. Thanks be to God.

My mother and Mrs Burke were great friends; they wore flowery aprons with white flour rubbed into the front. When my sister drank paraffin oil while my mother was at Benediction it was Mrs Burke who jumped the fence with the jam to make the child sick and save her life. We had to pray so hard after that. Before that we didn't pray hard enough.

Nighttimes stayed dark. We wore summer dresses as night clothes. We crossed our hands across our chests and we watched the shadows dance in the dying fire. We were terrified of the shadows and what came out of the shadows and we daren't look out for fear the Púca[4] would see you and call you into a different dimension.

When the dog let out a piercing howl you knew someone was going to die and if you heard the Banshee wailing you knew that person had died and it was someone that lived not too far away.

Cancer was feared as much as the Banshee. No one seemed to survive it then when the nights were darker. Cancer was described as a withering disease that made grown men look like babies in the coffin. He was shrunk and withered and he had brown crinkly skin. God bless the mark.

Whistling was good, but not if women did it; women had no place whistling or wearing slacks. Patrick Craven whistled on his way home every night. He whistled that famous tune from 'The Bridge on the River Kwai.' When he went to England and the whistling stopped, our lives changed for the worse.

The darkness loomed and stayed and no whistling anymore to make us feel secure in our beds. His whistling was the last sound we heard at night. Now we heard only the darkness calling us, the menacing dark with its heavy overcoat.

We were told often how we spoiled things, but we asked God fervently to forgive us our stupidity. We were told, too, to stop looking in the mirror in case the devil would look out at us. Terrify and be terrified, but God was always there to fall back on and offending God would not be tolerated. It was the greatest cloud of all, and in levels of darkness, it was by a mile the darkest.

The Púca

I asked my mother if it was a sign
of something that my Communion veil
was sticking to Judy Connors' at the altar.

Herself and Mrs Burke with their arms folded
under their big cushioned breasts
were giving harum-scarum glances and mar-dhea⁵ sighs.
They were at the start of a laughing session
that would end with tears being wiped away
by the tail end of their flowery aprons.

And why wouldn't it be a sign,
didn't my mother and her sisters in from Maree
talk in signs and piseogs⁶ all the time?
Every rickety move any Ballybrit bird made
was a sign of something or other.
Jackdaw, crow, magpie or maggot.

And if the goats shat on your dahlias
God knows who was going to get an airmail letter.
'God bless the mark' was used for everything, not just
when your neighbour's child had a strawberry birthmark
as big and bright as a peony rose.
And if anyone heard the Banshee's cry,
that was it, some poor devil was a goner.

Our days were one long piseog
and the Púca was there too to frighten the wits out of us.
It was the Púca you would meet in all his malevolence
when you found yourself at the bottom of the well
if you dared poke your snout out after dark.

But God, who never slept,
was always flung like holy water
during a thunder storm, between you and all harm,
and the Púca, like the cuckoo, could go and spit.

The Faraways

Going to Connemara in the car with a father, a father who knows Irish songs. He likes to lilt. I lilt to myself, I mime a lilt. The scenery cosies all the way up to the birds' loft and the sky pulls the curtains. 'Peigín Leitir Móir'[7] and 'An Poc ar Buile'[8] could get an airing. The omens are good, any minute now the Teanga Eile[9] might jump up and devour me. We drive into the relations' yard. The house is built on rock. We are beyond the place where road signs matter. This is not ring-a-rosary territory, this is read-a-face territory and read-the-eyes territory and read-the-oilskin-tablecloth.

The relations speak in tongues, full of sing, full of sorrow. The boulders watch every action and no action. A three-legged dog brings luck, a four-legged dog brings a spring lamb, the sunshine a blessing, the birds a song. Dread is a creaking gate in a neighbour's yard or an upturned wheelbarrow. Dread is difference. Dread is seeing the stars in the shape of a hunter. Dread is the black owl. Dread is an old woman's dream. Dread is a red-haired cailín on a boat.

I didn't know what a father was saying to the other two hand-clappers but they were laughing. They are going to give us boiled chicken and we better eat it quickly before the lingo devours it. It was a Sunday language without the holy water and a priest with foul breath and it had all afternoon for itself and us. The lilting was over for now. The sounds and the blissey-bliss was interwoven and it was all tied up in an old dishcloth. I couldn't reach any of it but I loved all of it. Afraid was there too, under a rock watching me. I'm a disturber.

Whoever she was, she was Boston-christened and they named her often. And they seemed to be able to see her because they kept looking out, the language rising and falling, the chicken dying to be eaten to spare them their loss. Every clock on the oilskin tablecloth told us what time 'The Faraways' got up and what time 'The Faraways' got the boat, but the oilskin tablecloth never said what time 'The Faraways' were coming home. That was that day and it went on for a week.

Another day, another Sunday, a father lilts: Di diddle di diddle diddle diddle diddle dum. In the car with a father. We are in tumble time, trees and houses are tumbling the wildcats. I want to cry but I mime a lilt instead. We are going to Connemara to visit his relations. A father stops lilting and starts singing 'Peigín Leitir Móir' and 'An Bhfaca Tú Mo Shéamuisín'[10] and then he goes quiet. He is having sad thoughts. Then he snaps out of it and he starts lilting again. I'm still in the tumble-dryer. I want to vomit, but I don't want to spoil things for a father. I'm a disturber.

You have to remember where you came from so that you will know how to go back. Here you are beyond road signs, and directions are only for whooper swans and swallows. A father lilts and follows the stone walls and reads the faces and the hands. The aunt and uncle come out to meet us again and they all burst into the language he loves and hates. The boulders watch every action, and no action ever staggers the boulders. They clock up every footfall, every blade of anxiety that surfaces when they start talking about 'The Faraways'.

Sometimes they give the deaf ear, but they are just letting on. The boulders never sleep.

I want to go to the toilet. I ask a father and they all burst out laughing, "You see that mountain, a chailín?[11] It's all yours." I am privileged to have such a toilet. I am privileged. A chailín likes the quietness.

After we eat the boiled chicken, they all look out. They look out a lot, same as the last visit. They are looking for 'The Faraways'. Where could they be? 'The Faraways' never come back to the place with no road signs. The other language is in full flight; they laugh and cry in it, and I know it's all about 'The Faraways'. 'The Faraways' did the devil's work by leaving.

This day a father decides that he is going to take me to see where his mother is buried. This is a treasure hunt. We get to the old graveyard and the boulders' uncles are spat out all over the place. I know that today there would be no 'Peigín Leitir Móir'. He can't find her. He tries this corner and that corner. She was buried just inside the wall. Which wall? I don't know one wall from the other. I mime a lilt. He tries all the corners. His face is red. She is gone with 'The Faraways'. But they went by boat. She went into the ground when a father was six months. There are no road signs or headstones, only broken ones or ones that slide down like a barrel in the bog. A father's mother is lost. We find no treasure. I feel sick. I am a disturber.

Back at the house the language my father loved and hated was getting a right battering. His father was a 'Faraway', but he came back once and had new boots and a suit for him. A father was happy. He thought: This is it, I'm outta here, good luck suckers. But a grandfather gave him to a farmer in Menlough to work his heart out until it was time for him to join the army.

A grandfather told the boat to wait and he jumped on it again and regained his status as a 'Faraway'. A father was below in Menlough, crying for a mother he never knew.

The treasure hunt ended badly. No sign of the mother who died when a father was six months. We were soon on the road with no signs. He didn't need directions. The stone walls were his map. The briars were his heather. His face was red. He didn't lilt. I didn't mime.

An Teanga Eile

Bhí mé i Leitir Móir
le m'athar
bhí mé óg, an-óg.
Bhí gaolta m'athair
ag labhairt i dteanga eile
bhí siad ag gáire i dteanga eile
bhí siad ag ól i dteanga eile
bhí siad ag tafann i dteanga eile
bhí siad ag argóint i dteanga eile
is nuair a tháinig an iomarca cainte faoin imirce
bhí siad ag caoineadh i dteanga eile.

The Other Language

I was in Leitir Móir
with my father
I was young, very young
my father's relations
were speaking in another language
they were laughing in another language
they were drinking in another language
they were barking in another language
they were arguing in another language
and when all the talk came up about emigration
they were crying in another language.

English Translation by Rita Ann Higgins

Crocodile Tears

My parents were in two places at the same time – they were out walking around the council estate we lived in and they were behind the wallpaper watching us running amok. We moved here from Baile Crua when I was eleven, and the most exciting thing was the flush toilet and the obscenity of having a toilet indoors. We are a few years here now and the novelty has worn off.

Why else, I ask you, would a father come back in such a rage, such a fire-devil red-faced rage, eyebrows-on-fire rage? He must have seen what we were doing even though he was out walking. We were óinseachs[12] and amadáns[13] and we ran amok.

"Yes, mother?" He called her mother sometimes. Probably because he couldn't find his mother's grave in Connemara that day we went looking when I was only a small óinseach.

"Are you ready for our walk?" They owned it, it was 'our' walk. When you hear 'our', you hear ownership even if you are only an óinseach. They went for a lovely Our Walk around Mervue.

Mammy would put on her olive green jacket, three-quarter-length sleeves, and always with a multicoloured diamond brooch. To us she looked like a princess. We loved every inch of her and her swollen ankles. He was thin enough to slide past limbo, he took shrapnel for his Confirmation. He never spared it like a wise one might do. A little bit of powder and lipstick when the olive green jacket went on, dark olive, rich and velvet smooth. A little lipstick, a dash of powder, not like what the trollops wore on television. The ones who were always screeching, annoying a father. Making him fire the shrapnel.

A father did not need to polish his shoes for the walk around the avenues. Pearse Avenue, Barry Avenue, McBride Avenue, Plunkett Avenue and McDermott Avenue and back up to where we lived, Parnell Avenue. Though polishing his shoes was quite a ritual, like cutting the hedge. He polished and shined. Mammy prayed and prayed for the grace of a happy death. We did the devil's work.

"See you later," and Mammy dipped her two fingers into the holy water font and blessed herself and sprinkled the rest onto the floor, making the sign of the cross with the left-over holy water on the floor. Never waste anything, especially holy water. Floors have to be blessed too, every amadán knows that.

They are gone out for a walk and it's now time for the amadáns and óinseachs to go berserk, running wild, fooling, messing, high jinks, blindman's bluff.

'Mimic a Father' was the most popular. *If I take off my belt to you you will feel it*. It was a great laugh, such a funny thing to say. Another funny 'Mimic a Father' game was my brother chasing me with the wooden crocodile, *come back here you striapach, don't you give me back cheek. I want front cheek and I want it now*. We laughed and laughed and why wouldn't we? It was always only pretending when my brothers did it. I only felt wild excitement at being chased, and no fear, well maybe a little fear.

The crocodile was brought back from the Congo by one of my brothers who was in the army. It was a hard crocodile. I didn't like the crocker and the crocker didn't like me. It was part of a pair. They were twins, but not really identical twins because one had his mouth open and the other one had his lips sealed. The sealed-lips crocker got misplaced, lost, stolen, went to limbo, whatever, but his brother stayed, because he liked the way it felt when it met the disturber's head.

They were out walking, and linking. My mother linked a father's arm. They looked like one person from behind, a person with four legs. One two-legs had lovely swollen ankles. I liked to see them walk down McDermott Avenue linking. They weren't in limbo. The amadáns were in limbo. A place you go before you see God or a place you go where you never see God. You could be in limbo for as long as the Children of Lir were on the lake freezing their tail feathers off. They were linked, they were connected. They were joined. If I could link with someone I would be saved. Link me. I want to be linked.

Even though they were out there walking, they were here too, behind the wallpaper. Why else would a father come back like a bull punctured in the eye with a knitting needle? The bull's eye. He bellowed. A deep breath in and it took him all of our childhood to let it out again.

"If I told you once, you amadáns, I told you a thousand times. Always draw the curtains when the lights are on!" Our big-fat-swollen-ankle sin. We didn't draw the curtains when the lights were on. We didn't deserve to see God. People would see what we didn't have. We had nothing but an empty shell with cupboards to match and a wooden crocodile, a hand-carved wooden crocodile to beat the back-answer daughter with. I'm a disturber. Link me.

Be Someone

For Christ's Sake,
learn to type
and have something
to fall back on.

Be someone,
make something of yourself,
look at Gertrudo Ganley.

Always draw the curtains
when the lights are on.

Have nothing to do
with the Shantalla gang,
get yourself a right man
with a Humber Sceptre.

For Christ's sake
wash your neck
before going into God's House.

Learn to speak properly,
always pronounce your ings.
Never smoke on the street,
don't be caught dead
in them shameful tight slacks,

spare the butter,
economise,

and for Christ's sake
at all times
watch your language.

Brides of the Stitch 'n Time

At the time I had no idea what the word 'multinationals' meant. The only thing I knew for certain was that it meant something big, some Super Mac thing that could not be bettered. The buntings were out, the multinationals are coming, Hurray Hurray. Get your backside out of that scratcher and go down to that new industrial estate and find yourself a job, a real job. The jobs were there for the taking. This was 70s Ireland and there were jobs aplenty in Mervue Industrial Estate. Everyone was singing the praises of the new industrial estate and the lovely multinationals. New words, easy to say words, slide off the tongue words, but a few short years later these would become hard to stomach words, dirty words, putrid words.

This was a very young, boy-chasing industrial-estate-tasting me. Wonder was the only fruit in town. These were the exciting days when the only priority was washing the hair and slapping on the layers of makeup. Sexy was the word made flesh that dwelt amongst us. It was in the oxygen and in the trees. Energy was the second prayer of the day. Have it, keep it, use it. Waste it at your peril. The industrial estate had its mechanical claws out for me and I embraced them with vigour and devil-may-care. Try our factory first, girl, and see what we have to offer, and if you don't like our factory go next door. We want you, we love you, slip inside and get addicted. The multinationals need you. Get Ireland off its knees with your young blood was the invisible slogan that lead us.

I got hooked on the chatter from the girls in the shirt factory, the stories about boys and dance halls and what went on in the backs of old cars after dances. The kissing stories, the telling-all stories. Someone was 'such a ride', someone else was 'the town bike'. Factory lore was enhanced with nods and glances, and an internal rhythm of licentiousness was palpable.

In reply to the question, "What was he really like?" the ultimate put down was when a little finger was exhibited and crooked into the shape of a worm. The repartee from the factory girls was honed and blade-like. No nearby male was exempt from the sharpness of the factory girl's tongue.

The girls would jive with each other in the factory toilet and the Tannoy system blasted out the popular songs all day long. Toilet breaks were taken often and it was also a chance for a quick fag and more dance hall stories. Magical times, half innocent, half pagan. We were the factory girls; we were cutters and stitchers and we were happy most of the time. The shirt factory had more females than males so that 'eager to seduce' pulse that rushed through our veins was heightened. You had to peacock or else you had your sewing machine where you sat and drifted into the land of tedium. The jivers were never bored.

I liked the pay packet too and when my mother took the house money out of it I was given my spending money. I went straight down to Dunnes to buy something new for the dance that weekend. Usually it would be something white because of the flourescent lighting in the Hangar ballroom. We all wore white. We looked like brides. We were brides of the stitch 'n time.

In the buckle factory, all the buckles were called after German rivers. On the outside we could slip 'the Oder' or 'the Danube' or 'the Rhine' into conversation and it gave us a sense of importance. The factory was very near our house in Mervue, but I never went home for lunch in case I would miss anything. I liked the buckle factory, but I missed the girls from the shirt factory.

I felt I had to taste as many factories as I could. Jobs were plentiful in Ireland and the industrial estate was the only show in town. I did the nut and washer factory after the buckle factory and I finally ended up in the crème de la crème of factories, Digital.

I arrived at spic-and-span Digital. More country girls and country lads, some townies. It was a community within a community. The factory floor was like a football pitch. This was Multi Multi. The conditions were great, everyone talked about the conditions. They had their own nurse, for God's sake.

The canteen was like a posh restaurant; it had juices and fresh fruit on display. I thought fresh fruit was only for patients in hospitals. No more squashed sandwiches in the bottom of your bag. The talk was all toasted ham and cheese sandwiches for the first break. I longed for the first break at around ten a.m. It was now 1977. Heather was in my belly, and I was always hungry. The company, like all the other multinationals, was good to work for but they didn't have any unions. Why in God's name would we need a union when the company was so good to us? Weren't they like family? At Christmas time they were bountiful. They would big-turkey you, and if you and your wife worked for Digital, they big-turkeyed you twice. You were fowled rightly, plucked, stuffed and roasted. You brought your own gravy.

Our turkey was so big it would not fit in the oven and we had to take a hatchet to it on Christmas Day. Key words were emerging: great company, big turkey, hatchet job. There was a 'no union' echo floating around the edge of the multinational roadshow. Why would you need a union when you had big turkeys? As we later learned, the big turkeys were the red herrings in the end.

I had my baby, Heather, in September, 1977. Half toasted ham and cheese, half multinational. Not long after that I started to hear 'pulling out stories'. The multinationals were going to other countries, where they didn't eat turkey. The multinationals made buckets full of money in Ireland because of a special love-in, big-turkey deal they had with the Irish government. As soon as the special incentives clock stopped ticking, the multinationals ran and took the money with them. They went to Morocco and South East Asia and other exotic sounding places and they never looked back.

Meanwhile a lot of the jiving girls married the country lads, and some of the townies married some of the locals, and they got big mortgages and had big babies after all the goodies the multinationals were throwing at them over the years. Now they were left with nothing but the jive and the magical lingo that first brought them together. At least when they rolled over to meet each other in the king size bed that they bought on the never-never when the goose was not yet cooked, they still had each other and a lot of happy memories. But as one of the girls from the shirt factory said to me one day in town outside Liptons, "Where can I cash that?"

When the Big Boys Pulled Out

In S.P. S.
we parted the nuts
we parted the washers
between this and lunch time
we smoked.

A nut in this barrel
a washer in that barrel
never a washer in with a nut
never a nut with a washer be.

After lunch
was much the same,
divide and conquer
nut and washer
no thought for cancer
we all smoked on.

We had plenty of
nut and washer jokes,
but they were all played out
and only used
when a new girl started.

We were cruel
sending her for a glass hammer,
a bucket of compressed air.
Soon enough she was flashing the ash,
and goading us on an all-out strike,
when we got dermatitis.
This decisive thinker won us over
in a hurry, making her part
of our nut and washer brigade.

Our fag breaks
became our summer holidays
when the Big Boys pulled out.

Now everything
was in the one barrel
butts, nuts, bolts,
washers, dryers,
eye shadows,
wedding dresses,
bell-bottoms,
hopes, dreams, fantasies,
platforms,
Beatlemania,

Costa del Sols,
where-will-you-get-work-now-jokes:
that were no jokes
Benidorums
all alore-ums.

Our fag breaks
became our summer holidays
when the Big Boys pulled out.
No further need
of our discretion
a nut here
a washer there.

Melancholy in the TB Ward

Melancholy was an unwelcome hawker that hung around the TB ward. It never dressed up, it just hung out in the carbon and mingled with us 'boney biddies'. Sometimes it just claimed us, no notice given, just smash and grab, not that there was anything to smash and precious little to grab. Other times it let on to be hope, throwing glossy reflections from mirrors that were never dusted. Dust was never far away. You were always reminded of where you were heading – Dustville.

Your image crumpled at every turn, sometimes you were so slight you could hardly catch a glimpse of yourself, not that you wanted to, but at least what the eye can see must be there in grey pyjamas and jam jaws. I see therefore I am.

I was twenty-two. My first-born was a few weeks old. They say pregnancy will bring things on. They say a lot of things. I could see the baby every week but only through the window of the sanitorium, her father propping her up and making her little hand wave at me. I never waved back. I was a looker. I looked and looked. One day she will have teeth, I will have wings.

Hyperbole and jelly was what we had. Mother of Mercy language, without verb or vibe. Just a roll-call of ancients who couldn't help us here because they only existed in a place with fluffy clouds where disease was a dirty word. Here the roof was rotting and the patients were wasting. No problem at all to see a fallen tooth on the corridor. The place belonged to the fallen.

It was obvious when a fellow spitter had been claimed by melancholy. The telling signs were when the two slices of thinly buttered bread were left uneaten and the eyes had that 'gone to bed' look, the eyes that gape but see nothing, the eyes that wear a 'just there' stare. Joy and mischief took a long weekend when melancholy got under our skin. It favoured our ward; it rarely left except when the priest was coming.

It vanished then for fear of the cross or the flying scapulars. It returned again midweek, or on rainy days with no stopping, or on foggy days. It loved the foggy days. It came in with the mist and let on to be something else; always a shape shifter, but melancholy was its maiden name. It was corner-of-the-eye present but absent in rhyme.

It could drag you into that dank forlorn place handmade for tuberculins. It could bully you like no other emotion. It called you negative and you answered back. I do. It called you miserable and you answered back. I do.

When melancholy left, you had to start all movement with a crawl. You never actually rose to the occasion but you did try. The danger with melancholy was that you got used to the starkness and the loneliness and there was a chance that you might want to hold onto it. At least you knew it, so therefore you felt. Feeling something, even something negative, was better than feeling nothing at all. We have seen the patients with the empty eyes. The misery you know is better than the misery you let on to know. Claim your misery and hug it tight. Give me back my misery, or make mine misery with a dash of mime.

We lived in the Rahoon flats when the doctor called up. He said, go directly to the San, do not pass Shantalla or the jean factory. Go straight there and take your streptomycin. Another voice said, look out at the cats and crows and the rotting cabbage, welcome to unit 9B, expect nothing and you won't be disappointed. Sweat to your heart's content, the hallucinogenic kick is delicious. Cover your mouth when you cough.

This is a TB ward not a crochet circle; face the wall when you cry. If you see two abandoned thin slices of bread on your neighbour's tray, walk the other way. Use your sputum mug early and often. Report all blood-spotted hankies, your own and others. Express no signs of gaiety, it's against house rules. If you want fresh air, go out with the cats and the crows. It won't cure your TB but it will put you in touch with your maternal side. Hug a scrawny cat and see how good it makes you feel. Hug a scrawny cabbage and see how ridiculous it makes you feel.

Then a father lands in with 'The Sentinel' and shows you that your friends are in jail. He says 'all your friends,' but the word *all* means nothing to you. You don't know how lucky you are to be in here getting three squares a day and a cot, and look at the views, mind you the cats and the cabbage don't look so hot, but have you ever seen a healthier looking bunch of crows? Don't tell anyone what you have. Tell them you have a bad cold. A bad cold can be anything. TB will always be TB.

Next morning, sister with the wings on her head tells us straight up that she wants to be able to see her face in our sputum. Get cleaning, she says, the priest is coming. Tidy those bedside lockers, polish those sputum mugs, get cracking, the priest is coming. We say in unison, "Yes, sister, we can feel it in our bones."

The Priest is Coming We Can Feel It in Our Bones

In the TB ward
we queue for the bath,
our bodies are knackered
we are all skin and bone,
but the priest will give us
the body of Christ.

(This isn't just hearsay
Sister Mary Mammary swears)

I'm the youngest here
except for the epileptic.
She throws a fit
at the drop of a hat,
rolls her eyes
and rattles her head.

For her tantrum
she'll get more of everything,
a spot of tea
a spot of toast
brown bread with
obscene amounts of butter,
sputum mugs full of glucose
white bread with
obscene amounts of butter.
You name it
we deserve it
she gets it
all for a fit a fortnight.

Our spot is on the lung.
We get to say ninety nine
ninety nine times
but no goodies
unless we rattle and roll.
Failing a fit
our phlegm talk
must be convincing,
otherwise we're out on our ear
with our bones in a bag.

The excitement is building
for the body of Christ,
our cheeks are flushed
our eyes are wide.

A pep talk
from Sister Mary Mammary –
to put zip in our loins
glucose in our mug.

"Come on now
he's landed,
throw shapes
not shadows,
and remember,
no shuffling
no profuse sweating
no farting
no acting the maggot
no fainting
no fits
and absolutely
no spitting."

The priest is coming
we can feel it in our bones.

A Future Pickled with Funerals

We had no past. Our memories were not our own. Our memories were all shoe-boxes and Halloweens and things sticking out of the top of wardrobes. Our pasts were before us in big plastic sandals that we never caught up with. We learned to fear fear, but there was a place for mischief and we all found that place and we milked it for what it was worth.

We lived beside the racecourse and we counted the days until the end of next July when the races started again. *Hup, hup a capaillín, hup hup again, you wouldn't sell a capaillín for nine pounds ten.*

Imperfect days were made dreamy, with Bull's Eyes and Peggy's Legs, and hot tar to walk in, and chase and be chased, but it was hard to keep down the nettles.

We were bobby-socks and clean your ears and cut knees and wear summer dresses in bed types, and some selfish children needed a reason to cry. So we had funerals and they were good for that. A good funeral meant a good cry. You could cry and cry and cry. Cry me a ferret. Cry me a field of nettles. Cry me an ice cream.

When the headmistress was laid out we saw our first dead body. She looked a bit like our mother, the same stature, the same plumpness. All the mothers looked like this except maybe the sister-in-law of the woman who came around like Ariel. She had no flesh on her cheeks. She had the nerves and she ran everywhere. "She is like a ferret," I heard a man say when I was waiting at the counter in O'Meara's for the Bull's Eyes. Men always used words like 'ferret' and 'a right trollop'. If a woman wasn't a 'ferret' she was 'a right trollop' and if she wore slacks she was 'a right trollop'.

My mother would die before she would call another woman 'a right trollop'. She would say 'ferret' and she would say 'the nerves'. The nerves were under every bush waiting to attack anyone who did not run fast enough to get away from the nettles and their past that had not yet happened.

The headmistress wasn't even my headmistress; she taught my brothers and sisters. At her wake the floors smelt of a lovely soothing wax. The smell stayed with me forever. It became the past I never had. She was the first corpse we saw and we could cry and cry and cry. Everyone has to pay for everything and we had to pay our respects. Go and pay your respects. We horsed around, and then at some point the bubble bursts and you look straight at the dead person and life is never the same. You mark this as the first person that you have seen laid out.

No amount of orange squash and pennies and pats on the head from grown-ups will obliterate the elephant in the room. Clock up the dead because it will never be a cake walk; in death the dead have their own dead personalities. It will be a ferret that never stopped running and it will affect the nerves.

The death of animals mattered too and was another reason to cry and cry. The weeping went on for days when Rebel was poisoned. The women made a circle around the dog's grave and cried. The crying can be with sadness or without sadness. I liked it with shit loads of sadness. Sadness is good. Stay sadness stay.

A neighbour's child died; a car ran over him. There was talk that his head was squashed, but he never ate his porridge and his head was small. The car went right over him, leaving him one perfect head. His injuries were substantial, his puddings were hanging in and his heart was hanging out.

Welcome back sadness, your loss was my loss. The car was grey and the sheet that covered the whole street was red. We knew what his knees were like and his shoes and his small shoulders. We played ball with him every day after school, but he ran out after the ball, and the ball got away.

My mother said "Run after God but never run after the ball. Let the ball run away. Your dreams can be made up of other chases, say the wind, say the moon, say the blackbird, say the rabbit, say the hare." We had a four or five or six year old reason to cry and cry, floods of tears, and he was buried in the graveyard near the racecourse, near enough to watch us play.

What I chased had no name or face or birth certificate. Some days I chased a bag of wind, other days it landed on my shoulders, a sack of coal. Shape shifters and ferrets under every bush. I had no past, I only had a future pickled with funerals.

A grandad brought Smarties on St Stephen's Day. A grandad was a father's father. He had two crutches. It was time for him to die, but not until the dog howled and my mother said the word 'piercing': 'piercing cries of the dog'. We had half-past-twos and half-past-threes and nothing ever added up. If someone was sick and our parents used the dark words and you stacked them up on top of one another, you would get a half past and one funeral and a good reason to cry.

Dark words were 'slack' and 'weaker' and 'not worth a ten bob note'. If you heard 'not worth a ten bob note', you knew there was no hope. Say not the cry of the banshee. Say not the guard coming to your door with a telegram. Say not the tinker woman putting a curse or the bad eye. Say not the Lord's name in vain. Do not the devil's work.

When President Kennedy died, the mothers cried, but it just didn't have the same effect on our puddings. I couldn't see it, and I needed a grey car to feel it or a grandad with crutches. Paint me the pictures, and I will cry you a dead dog or a little lad under a grey car. In truth, sometimes I didn't need pictures. I just needed the big wave to creep into the house and seek me out, and I would cry for Jesus and for me. There was a place for sadness and a place for Jesus. Sadness had bigger shoes than Jesus sometimes.

And then you were a big girl, and the sadness got fatter, and bits from your insides were falling out. Your puddings were nowhere to be found; maybe an old dog ate them on the roadside. You hoped that you wouldn't lose any more of your insides because, after a while, you knew if they threw a penny into you, the whole twelve cottages heard it rattling around.

I did forbid my mother to die, but you might as well be talking to the wall. I'm sixteen, I told her. I need a mother to tell me that red is nice on me. Wait till I'm twenty-something or thirty-something or wait till I'm forty-something and I could go with you.

My father could die at any time, but he hung around to remind me who was boss. I am the boss of everything. I was a sergeant in the army. Still, the night he died, I tossed and turned and was full of all the negatives that wear ghoulish get-ups and riddle the dreams. I couldn't wake. My sister was banging on the door to tell me, "Dad is dead, Dad is dead." "Dad who?" I said.

And when friends die, the baggage is less, but the loss can be more at some levels; or at least the loss seems greater because it is allowed. You can be heartbroken for friends. You can never really open the floodgates of true grief for a sibling or a parent or a nephew. They may as well just lock you up if you do that. Have a good bawl, but hold back on the grief, honey.

Jack Mitchell, the old commie, the only communist and absent-verb spotter in Mervue. He was a scholar. He gave me some of the books from his library. A few books, but such a legacy. He was always quoting other writers. He loved Robbie Burns and Shakespeare, and the 'A Drunk Man Looks At A Thistle' man. I would give him my essays for the Women's Studies diploma course and ask him to read them and check for howlers. He rang one day and said, "Every sentence must have a verb." Fine time to tell me. Are you sure? No one mentioned this before. I think he made it up. How could I get this far without a verb or a past? He had to go and die for himself, didn't he?

Anne Kennedy. Godmother to our Jennifer. She died, but not before we were all made to feel like we were her only friends. She taught us all about the second-hand shop and half-portions in the Corrib Restaurant and the literatures of the world. She once asked in the Credit Union if she could speak to the Board of Directors. What a laugh! One of the many books she gave me was *Moby Dick*. Anyone who gives you *Moby Dick* has to be watched.

She's on the high seas now. Her legacy was opening all those books, and quoting, and knowing like Jack. She knew things, rakes of things. She wore the sun every day and she looked chocolate straight in the face. Anne never knew what boring was and she could interpret our dreams. She did this often when we went to her confessional.

My nephew Michael was eighteen, nearly nineteen. His sadness was huge sometimes, and then he would bounce back, and we would have him for another little while. But he got the 'flu and the black dog visited him that weekend as well, and that was the end of it. Michael is with me a lot of the time. He has a nephew's pass, he can come and go in my thoughts and dreams anytime he likes. I wish he had stayed.

I took Communion for the first time in thirty years on the night of Michael's tenth anniversary mass in his mother's house and I didn't burst into flames. Mind you, as I walked home, I thought I felt scorch marks under my feet.

My brother Tony worked in Saudi Arabia for years as an engineer. When he came home on leave, I always seemed to meet him in the same places, in Shop Street or the Eyre Square Centre, strolling with his wife Joan. A chance for us to have a cup of tea and catch up. "How are your girls doing?" Always warning me about that big mouth of mine. Every encounter was memorable in a different way, but laughter was the common denominator. I'd say to him, "This is a coincidence." He'd say to me, "Listen Rita, listen love, there are no coincidences, no chance encounters. And by the way, how are you, really?"

In 2004, I went on a walking holiday to the Czech Republic. Walking, talking, laughing, drinking at night. On our day off we crossed over on a day trip to Dresden, to see how the city had been rebuilt after the bombings by the Allied Forces during the Second World War. We weren't laughing then. The city was restored to its former glory, but it was a graveyard for too many.

My room in the hotel was in the basement and I had no mobile coverage. Glad to get to my bed, I fell into a deep sleep, helped, I'm sure, by the two brandies I had had in the room of a female companion earlier.

Sometime later a loud knocking woke me. A man's voice: "Rita, open the door, I have a message for you." I recognised his married voice; his wife a walking companion. What was he doing at my door at two a.m.?

I decided to ignore him, hoping he would stroll back to his own cot soon. I could give him daggers at breakfast. He wouldn't go away; he kept calling me, kept knocking. I shouted out "Go away," like you would to a nuisance dog.

"Rita, can you open the door. I have a message for you! Your sister has been trying to contact you. Something has happened to your brother in Saudi Arabia." I opened the door.

Unadorned

In a room in Shannon airport
where no one lived,
we looped the box
he came home in
a box with a number
none of us knew.

I Am A Goose On One Leg

The waiting area in Malaga airport is limited, so if you have two hours to kill a quiet corner to yourself is a bit ambitious. I have a good book and a cup of tea, so on a pleasure scale I'm doing pretty good already. It is noisy, though, and there does not seem to be any place for the noise to go. It hangs in the air over your head. It's very loud and raucous and when the sounds beat off each other, it takes on a surreal quality, more like squawking birds doing battle than people chatting.

At intervals, people start pouring out of arrivals and falling into the arms of their loved ones. I had no idea that watching people greeting could be such a moving experience. I watched every loving collision as it happened.

I found myself thinking about the curious intimacy of the hug, its safe and reassuring effect. Some huggers are so passionate it makes me tearful. It's so real, and spontaneous. Some huggers make your breathing change to an uneven beat. I started to think about good huggers. Do I know any good huggers? Can I remember the best hug I've ever had? Some huggers hoop as well as hug. Some huggers clap the recipient on the back as well as hug. So many emotions are running side by side; they are reflected on the faces of those waiting for the loved ones to walk through that door. The emotions vary from fear and anxiety to pure joy.

I'm thinking about a hug I once had that lasted what seemed like an eternity, but it probably wasn't for very long. It was tender and secure, with a clear message of friendship. It was never topped.

Some get hugged, and some are huggers. Some might be great huggers but not while they have an audience. Some huggers need an audience. Often people break rank and run under the fence, usually grandmothers on seeing their loving grandchildren.

At Malaga airport you are allowed to bring your dog in, and there is nothing like the excitement a dog displays when it sees its owner walking through those doors.

Dogs aside, the lovers' hug is an entirely different matter. They hug and kiss and stand back and 'let me look at you' and more hugs and more kisses. You can tell the lovers a mile off. When teenagers meet here they flock-hug and almost spin each other into San Pedro. They are loud, but this time it's a nice loud, an approved-of loud.

The reason why someone waits at arrivals in an airport is pretty obvious, but the strange mechanisms and energy that floats around as you hug or immediately after you are embraced is not so easy to define. The most striking and powerful action when people are hugging is that arms are outstretched to draw a loved one closer for a flash-lightening second or seconds, seconds that can never ever be measured in real time. The hug is an action that may not warrant another thought, a phenomenon that brings about closeness, something intangible which enhances our ability to give and receive affection.

Thoughts haven't time to finish themselves. Chaos and giddiness set in. The arrival doors are opened, and they're off. Some time ago, I came across this quote, but I don't know who wrote it. It takes four hugs a day to survive, eight hugs a day to maintain, and twelve hugs a day to grow.

Malaga O' Malaga

I am a goose on one leg
waiting at Malaga airport.
No one will notice that I'm a goose
because Malaga airport is full of geese
standing on one leg
and it's always the left leg.

The noise at Malaga airport has a
cadence, a loud loud lisp
and a cac cac cackle,
all thunder no rain.
Some noises are necessary
if we want to see the other birds
and we all want to see the other birds.
We have to put up with the noise.
Aren't we making half the noise ourselves,
so many geese together
so many wild geese.

I stick my neck out,
I have a neck like a swan,
a shrink once told me.
My father used to say
I had a neck for anything but soap.
I stick my neck out to see
if the other bird has landed.
The rest do the same thing,
they stick their necks out.

The odd cratur hops on the other foot
but we take no notice,
hardly anyone hisses
except two old codgers
who fell fowl of the flock years ago.
They were leaning against the back wall
complaining about air miles
and the journey south,
scratching their tail feathers.

You could forgive them that,
this waiting is wearing on the nerves,
loved ones are coming for Christmas,
the expectations terrify,
the noise is now more whooper than hubbub.
It blocks out everything
except what the eyes can see.
All the eyes are on the arrivals gate
and on the electronic notice board
landed, delayed, landed, delayed,
landed, delayed, landed,
which is it, which is it,
we all stretch our swan necks.

It's hardly a sanctuary here
but all those open arms
harness their own remedy,
a vein-less thread-less remedy
that needs no water or air to flourish
just those outstretched arms
and a dash of something
unseen unheard
made from lonely
made from loss.

We were alone for nine hundred years,
now all those loving collisions
are turning us into right ninnies,
we are sobbing and bobbing
and all over happy and sad and secure
but our clothes are all creased
and the teenagers aren't goslings anymore
but they are still whooping
and the noise is all thunder no rain
people are getting hugged
right left and centre, arms outstretched
loving collisions are happening
feathers are flying
all over Malaga airport.

Toronto Interlude

How does a poem start, and how do you bring it to fruition? Who knows for sure. In my opinion, how or where the poem begins has more to do with being receptive when the poem vein starts to leak thoughts slantways, or sideways, or anyways, when ideas come with a new crispness, when words have a ping in their step, or when sounds evoke a memory that may be long forgotten.

Sometimes when I arrive at a new place, the wonder of that place takes over and my antennae are out for any creative crumbs that might be floating in the atmosphere.

About two years ago I was in Toronto giving a reading. It was my first time there. The hotel we stayed in was kind of posh, and we were delighted with the comfort. When we went out for a walk the most striking thing we noticed was that most of the people we saw nearby were struggling in one way or another.

The doorman at the hotel had a comic way about him. His body movements were swift, he would stop mid-step and change direction, a bit like Groucho Marx. His eyes darting, he had every direction scanned. He seemed to bounce when he walked; he did a kind of pirouette. He always had a wad of money that he spread out like a fan in front of his face (he wouldn't do that in parts of the Galway I know and love!). It was a peacock display thing, as if to say, "I'm Flash Harry, look at me."

We got the distinct impression that Flash Harry did not like us. We were not nice luggage people, we had no Gucci labels, we were haversackers. When we needed information about anything, we were told "Ask The Concierge".

Every time we went out we saw the same people: strung out or scarred by poverty, or some other sadness. It was like walking down the avenue of loss.

When I got back to Ireland, the people I had seen in Toronto near the hotel, and the Concierge, were jostling for position in the alleyways of my mind. They were side by side, yet Niagaras apart. A poem was starting, or a couple of lines were colliding, and they would not go away. It was up to me to follow it through or let it go.

When I start writing a poem I'm not worried if the first draft does not have a sense or structure about it; it's just to get the bare bones down. It doesn't take much shape until around the third or fourth draft. By then I have a fair idea what I'm after.

I'm pleased when I get what I think is a good line. If the opening stanza is not as strong as other stanzas, I start writing it out again. Punctuation has always been problematic for me. I try not to have too many full stops because they are so sudden, and they halt things, and I like the rhythm to go from the start to the end, and full stops play puck with the rhythm.

I had never seen a black squirrel before, and they were plentiful in Toronto. I put 'black squirrels galore' in the notebook. I might be able to tie it in someway. Having loads of notes won't make you ready, but notes can prompt you about things you have forgotten. So, yes, the notebook is important.

"Some poems write themselves," the soothsayers say. I don't believe that. Poems have to be worked on, until you have done as much as you can to make all parts of the poem seem like a seamless piece.

Reading other people's work is very important, not just for the pleasure but for learning about technique and style.

Put the odd poem in the rubbish bin – it's tough but it's humbling to know that not all your poems will make the final cut.

I usually find when I have lost all interest in the poem, then it's finished. This generally happens after I have been rewriting and tinkering with it for about two weeks.

It's a combination of the gut, the heart, the mind, the notebook – then the hard work starts.

Ask The Concierge

The demented walk tricky step here
jittery footfall, fractious jibe.
They bicker in the 'everything for a dollar shop.'
Later when the energy is spent
they sit with their own selves
their underweight psyche.

One begs outside a shop called 'Seduction'
underwear to raise the Titanic
healthy looking mannequins with brazen breasts
balefuls of Canadian promise.
They come hither you but you never come hither them.
Their chilling look deceptive, their cherry lips,
kiss me kiss me, but only in your dreams loser.

Further down the street of the black squirrel
a shop owner boasts about the underground,
you should see our underground
safest in the world, no one ever gets plugged here.
In a doorway above Hades, a policeman tells a man with no legs,
my name is zero tolerance, have you a license for that rig?
My name is zero tolerance, where is your mud guard?

The concierge has the real power here
he takes one look at your luggage, one look at you
haversacks disgust him,
owners and trainers of haversacks disgust him more.
Cross him and you will never see one drop of Niagara fall.
He wide steps and side eyes you,
in his loose suit, hair oil up his sleeve,
his feet are made of sponge.
He deals in looks and eyebrow raising
the Concierge code, uncrackable to the luggage losers.

Back down on Loss Avenue
I ask the man outside 'Seduction' if I can take his picture.
Don't ask me, I have no picture to give or take,
what you see is what you get, you see nothing you get less.

What the concierge seeks he finds
he pirouettes, he plucks, he spins, he flies
where the concierge lives, the beggar dies.

Easy Peasy Bóithrín[14] and Bog

Waking up in Spiddal and seeing the Cliffs of Moher and the Burren from the bed is a pleasant enough start to any day. A little to my right I can see the Aran Islands. My father once told me that he had never been to the Aran Islands even though he had grown up in Leitir Móir in south Connemara.

I don't believe that the lack of travel limits the imagination. When you settle, the journey doesn't stop there. I knew a woman who lived in Prospect Hill, about two minutes from the centre of Galway city, and she used to say, "I'm going to Galway today." Since I moved to Spiddal this year, I have become the woman from Prospect Hill.

When I'm in Spiddal a nicer me sneaks out. The first thing Spiddal gives me is a deep contentment and it's often carried over from day to day. After I've been away giving a workshop or a reading I like nothing better than to fantasise about heading back to Spiddal. I usually ring my co-conspirator and find out what time he'll be arriving and we decide what I might cook.

I love to cook here. At home himself did the cooking for years while I was acting out the role of poet without a roadmap or a song. In Spiddal there is something illicit about cooking a huge dinner for the one who arrives with more plants and news from the city all of twelve miles away. I bake like the woman from *The Butcher Boy*. Buns everywhere.

I would have taken that Spiddal road many times as a child accompanying my father on his visits to relations in Léitír Móir. I don't remember much about the landscape only that you could always see the sea. I do remember the language they used was different and more passionate to the one we used at home. My relations spoke as if they were singing, the rhythms rising and falling. Sometimes I wondered if a big argument was going on, then with the next breath they would burst out laughing and start all over again.

Spiddal was not yet in the frame, it was still in that out-there place, the place without roads or birds and little or no links to my imagination.

Later I attended several Irish language courses in Carraroe. After the courses I didn't practise using the language enough, with the result that my spoken Irish was always fairly poor. So, for as long as I can remember, I knew that I would have to go back on the Connemara journey, back to where those mesmerising sounds came from. The Irish language was always going to be a pivotal force in me coming to Spiddal.

When I got here the first thing I did was ring the Údaras and find out what classes were available. That first week I joined in that ciorcal cómhrá[15] in the Crúiscín Lán. It isn't just an Irish circle, it is a social occasion that I have come to cherish. Tuesday nights are something to look forward to. They start up again in the autumn.

The Spiddal birds sing every morning, regardless of the weather. They never sing out of tune. They always sing out of season. They do weekends and bank holidays. They make holy days holier with their heart-warming chorus. When the birds sing, I believe in God. My heart melts, and I swear I'll be a better person. I lie. By the end of the day I might have clocked up a few resentments or a few negative thoughts about some unsuspecting soul who may have crossed me twenty years ago in a bus queue or at a Donovan concert.

One day towards the end of February I was in the box room taking a short break from throwing the IMPAC books at the cat.[16] I saw this tiny ad in a local paper that read, "House for Rent in Spiddal".

I didn't discuss it with anyone; I just rang the number and the woman at the other end of the line was warm and not at all greedy and the rest is history.

It's easy to be more interested in nature here because it's all around you. The other day I was walking down toward the pier, and I saw two pheasants pottering about the field, totally oblivious to my prying.

Another time I saw a fox, a beautiful fox with no look of slyness about him, he was right across from the cottage. I blinked, and he was gone. I find myself thinking about the fox, wondering when I'll see him again.

I rang himself and told him I saw the fox. Congratulations, he said, give yourself a big hug and spin the wheel.

I hope the fox doesn't find out about the pheasant sisters down by the pier.

The growth here is phenomenal, the lushness and the colour gives Spiddal a tropical island quality. You see nothing but purples and blues and velvety foliage, blackberries and raspberries, and buckets of blooming heather.

Máire in the library helps me find the Máirtín Ó Cadhain short stories in Irish and English. I go to the cottage and spend three hours reading one of his stories, crossing back and forth from the Eoghan Ó Tuairisc translations.

Joyce is the other Ó Cadhain. Ó Cadhain is such a complex and hugely challenging writer. An Gaelacadamh put on a series of lectures in Spiddal about his life and writing earlier this year, and I was fortunate enough to be able to attend some of them. Of course, you could read Ó Cadhain anywhere, but reading him in Spiddal somehow fits for me because of his links with Cois Farraige and the fact that I'm a cross between a tourist and a townie.

The library costs so little a year, and you can also access the internet there. Visiting the library is another social occasion that gives me an opportunity to speak Irish. Another thing about Spiddal is, I like to overhear children speak Irish to their parents on the street and in the supermarket.

I love the stillness that falls over the place at around seven in the evening when I'm walking down to the pier. The hubbub that bruised the serenity barrier earlier has melted and the place has a surreal quality again.

Here I have good neighbours who leave organic vegetables at my door.

I like that the pubs are all within walking distance from the cottage. Tigh Hughes has that 'something is about to happen' feeling about it and when Johnny Connolly, King of the Melodeon, starts coaxing that button box of his, something magical always happens. Music is the first language here. Johnny Connolly is like Francis Thompson's hound of heaven chasing the hare of your soul across the bridge of eternity.

In the bog, we walk and talk and sometimes we walk and don't talk. At first sight, the bog has little going for it in terms of paint and powder. It has a T-junction that leads nowhere in particular, but you always hang a right and follow the emptiness. The backdrop is of Quixote's giants offering signs of trespass and woe. You come to love the starkness. Out of that emptiness comes a stillness that is not inhabited with emotion or memory; no dash of pain. The stillness falls over the place, and it falls all over you. The bog is the place for losing and finding yourself.

Borders

There's no hope of a joy rider here
no one wears broken glass on their back walls
here there are no back walls
no front walls, no fences with menaces
no Rottweilers, no child-eating Dobermans
no pinch of tension in the air
that sets fire to a good night's sleep
no jumpiness that incites the joints
to early arthritis.

This is Pheasantville
easy peasy, bóithrín and bog
warbler boulevard
meander lane the pace the same
the borders here are invisible
you'll find them rarely in the bend of a look
the vexed angle of a grin
the crew cut greeting,
the verb that takes longer to pall.

NOTES

1. *Baile Crua* – hard town
2. *Straois* – grimace, grin
3. *Striapach* – a harlot, fornicator, prostitute, whore
4. *Púca* – a pooka, a sprite or ghost
5. *Mar-dhea* – as if
6. *Piseog* – superstition, a charm, or spell
7. *Peigín Leitir Móir* – Peggy Lettermore, Irish Song
8. *An Poc ar Buile* – The Mad Puck Goat, Irish song
9. *An teanga eile* – the other language or the other tongue
10. *An Bhfaca Tú Mo Shéamuisín* – Did You See My Seamuseen, Irish song
11. *A chailín* – a young girl
12. *Óinseach* – fool (female)
13. *Amadán* – fool (male)
14. *Bóithrín* – a boreen, narrow by-road, a lane, a small road
15. *Ciorcal cómhrá* – group who meet for Irish conversation/ lit. conversation circle
16. In 2005 Rita Ann Higgins was a judge of the IMPAC fiction prize.

About the Author

RITA ANN HIGGINS was born in 1955 in
Galway, Ireland. She is one of thirteen
children. Her first five poetry collections
were published by Salmon: *Goddess on
the Mervue Bus* (1986); *Witch in the Bushes*
(1988); *Goddess and Witch* (1990); *Philomena's
Revenge* (1992); and, *Higher Purchase* (1996).
Bloodaxe Books published her next three
collections: *Sunny Side Plucked* (1996);
An Awful Racket (2001); and *Throw in the
Vowels: New & Selected Poems* in May 2005 to mark her 50th
birthday. *Throw in the Vowels* was reissued in 2010 by Bloodaxe
with an accompanying CD of poems read by Rita Ann Higgins.
Her plays include: *Face Licker Come Home* (Salmon 1991); *God of
the Hatch Man* (1992), *Colie Lally Doesn't Live in a Bucket* (1993);
and *Down All the Roundabouts* (1999). In 2004, she wrote a
screenplay entitled *The Big Break.* In 2008 she wrote a play, *The
Empty Frame,* inspired by Hanna Greally, and in 2008 a play for
radio, *The Plastic Bag.* She has edited: *Out the Clara Road: The
Offaly Anthology* in 1999; and *Word and Image: a collection of poems
from Sunderland Women's Centre and Washington Bridge Centre*
(2000). She co-edited *FIZZ: Poetry of resistance and challenge,* an
anthology written by young people, in 2004. She was Galway
County's Writer-in-Residence in 1987, Writer-in-Residence at
the National University of Ireland, Galway, in 1994-95, and
Writer-in-Residence for Offaly County Council in 1998-99.
She won the Peadar O'Donnell Award in 1989 and has received
several Arts Council of Ireland bursaries. She was Green Honors
Professor at Texas Christian University in October 2000. Her
collection *Sunny Side Plucked* was a Poetry Book Society
Recommendation. She was made an honorary fellow at Hong
Kong Baptist University in November 2006. She divides her time
between Galway City and Spiddal, County Galway. Bloodaxe
will publish a new collection of her poetry, *Ireland Is Changing
Mother,* in 2011.

Photo: Christy Higgins